Ganga
Chalisa

Published in Sanskriti Press
by Rupa Publications India Pvt. Ltd 2025
7/16, Ansari Road, Daryaganj
New Delhi 110002

Sales centres:
Bengaluru Chennai
Hyderabad Jaipur Kathmandu
Kolkata Mumbai Prayagraj

Edition copyright © Rupa Publications India Pvt. Ltd 2025

All rights reserved.
No part of this publication may be reproduced, transmitted,
or stored in a retrieval system, in any form or by any means,
electronic, mechanical, photocopying, recording or otherwise,
without the prior permission of the publisher.

P-ISBN: 978-93-7003-300-9
E-ISBN: 978-93-7003-701-4

First impression 2025

10 9 8 7 6 5 4 3 2 1

Printed in India

This book is sold subject to the condition that it shall not, by way of
trade or otherwise, be lent, resold, hired out, or otherwise circulated,
without the publisher's prior consent, in any form of binding or cover
other than that in which it is published.

Contents

Introduction / 5

Chalisa / 7

आरती श्री गंगाजी / 94

Aarti Shri Gangaji / 95

Introduction

The Ganga Chalisa is a revered devotional hymn dedicated to the sacred river Ganga, a symbol of purity, divine grace, and spiritual nourishment. Composed in praise of this life-giving river, the Chalisa extols the divine qualities of the Ganga, which, according to Hindu belief, has the power to cleanse the soul and bring blessings to those who revere her. The Ganga, which flows from the peaks of the Himalayas, is considered the holiest of rivers, and the Ganga Chalisa serves as a reminder of its significance in both physical and spiritual realms.

The Ganga Chalisa, is structured in a traditional forty-verse format, where each verse highlights different aspects of the river's divine nature. The lyrics of the Chalisa evoke vivid imagery of the Ganga's journey, from its source in the Himalayas to its union with the plains, bringing life and vitality to the land. As with many devotional hymns, the verses not only describe the river's greatness but also offer prayers for purification and blessings, invoking Ganga's protection and grace for the devotee's well-being.

The tone of the Ganga Chalisa is deeply spiritual and meditative, and the words flow with a sense of reverence and awe. Each verse calls upon the Ganga to cleanse the devotee of sins, providing a means for spiritual salvation. The rhythm of the Chalisa enhances its devotional power, making it a popular prayer among devotees who seek peace, prosperity, and liberation from life's struggles. Recited with devotion, the Ganga Chalisa holds the promise of inner peace and connection to divine forces, resonating with those who believe in the river's transformative powers.

For centuries, the Ganga has been a vital part of Indian spirituality, and the Ganga Chalisa beautifully encapsulates this deep-rooted reverence for the river. Whether performed as part of a formal ritual or in the solitude of personal devotion, the Ganga Chalisa serves as a spiritual companion, offering solace and reminding the devotee of the river's eternal presence in the heart of India. Through its verses, the river is not only a physical entity but a symbol of divine grace, blessing, and continuous renewal.

Chalisa

॥ चौपाई ॥

जय जय जय जग पावनी,
जयति देवसरि गंग ।
जय शिव जटा निवासिनी,
अनुपम तुंग तरंग ॥

Jai jai jai jag pāvanī,
Jayati devsari gang.
Jai Shiv jaṭā nivāsinī,
Anupam tung taraṅg.

Victory, victory, victory to the sacred
mother of the world,
Victory to the divine river, the Ganga.
Victory to the one who resides in Lord
Shiva's matted hair,
Unmatched are her towering waves.

।। दोहा ।।

जय जय जननी हराना अघखानी ।
आनंद करनी गंगा महारानी ।।

Jai jai jananī harānā aghakhānī,
Ānand karanī Ganga Mahārānī.

Victory, victory to the mother who
removes all sins,
The Ganga, the queen of joy and bliss.

जय भगीरथी सुरसरि माता ।
कलिमल मूल डालिनी विख्याता ॥

Jai Bhagirathī surasari mātā,
Kalimala mūl ḍālinī vikhyātā.

Victory to Bhagirathi, the divine river mother,
Known for uprooting the root of sin in the Kali Yuga.

जय जय जहानु सुता अघ हनानी ।
भीष्म की माता जगा जननी ॥

Jai jai Jahānu sutā agha hanānī,
Bhīṣma kī mātā jagā jananī.

Victory, victory to the mother of the
world who removes all sins,
The mother of Bhishma, the universal
mother.

धवल कमल दल मम तनु सजे ।
लखी शत शरद चंद्र छवि लजाई ।।

Dhaval kamal dal mam tanū saje,
Lakhī shat sharad chandra chhavi lajaī.

My body is adorned with the pure white lotus petals,
As the hundred autumn moons feel shy of their radiance.

वहां मकर विमल शुची सोहें ।
अमिया कलश कर लखी मन मोहें ॥

Vahān makar vimal shuchī sohen,
Amiya kalash kar lakhī man mohen.

There, the crocodile (symbolizing purity) shines brightly and clean,
With an amrita (nectar) vessel in hand, it captivates the heart of the observer.

जड़िता रत्ना कंचन आभूषण ।
हिय मणि हर, हरानितम दूषण ।।

Jaditā ratnā kanchan ābhūṣaṇ,
Hiy maṇi har, harānitam dūṣaṇ.

Adorned with gems and golden jewellery,
The heart's jewel is Lord Hari, free from all impurities.

जग पावनी त्रय ताप नासवनी ।
तरल तरंग तुंग मन भावनी ॥

Jag pāvanī tray tāp nāsavānī,
Teral tarang tung man bhāvanī.

The one who purifies the world, who removes the three types of afflictions, With her flowing waves, she delights the mind, rising like a towering wave.

जो गणपति अति पूज्य प्रधान ।
इहूं ते प्रथम गंगा अस्नाना ॥

*Jo Gaṇapati ati pūjya pradhān,
Ihun te pratham Gaṅgā asnānā.*

The one who is most revered and central, Lord Ganapati,
Is followed by the first bath in the sacred Ganga.

ब्रह्मा कमंडल वासिनी देवी ।
श्री प्रभु पद पंकज सुख सेवि ॥

Brahmā kamaṇḍal vāsinī devī,
Śrī prabhu pad pankaj sukh sevī.

The goddess who resides in Brahma's water pot,
She who serves the lotus feet of Lord Shri with joy.

साथी सहस्त्र सागर सुत तरयो ।
गंगा सागर तीरथ धरयो ।।

Sāthī sahastr sāgar sut tarayo,
Gaṅgā sāgar tīrath dharayo.

The companion of a thousand seas, the son of the ocean,
He who carries the sacred Ganga and the holy pilgrimage.

अगम तरंग उठ्यो मन भवन ।
लखी तीरथ हरिद्वार सुहावन ॥

Agam taraṅg uṭhyo man bhavan,
Lakhī tīrath Haridwār suhāvan.

A profound wave arose, stirring the heart,
As one beholds the beautiful pilgrimage of Haridwar.

तीरथ राज प्रयाग अक्षैवेता ।
धरयो मातु पुनि काशी करवत ॥

Tīrath rāj Prayāg akṣaīvetā,
Dharyo mātṛ puni Kāśī karavat.

The king of all pilgrimages, Prayag, is imperishable,
The mother again holds Kashi in her embrace.

धनी धनी सुरसरि स्वर्ग की सीढ़ी ।
तरनी अमिता पितु पड़ पिरही ॥

Dhanī dhanī surasari svarg kī sīdhī,
Taranī amītā pitu paṛ pirahī.

Blessed is the divine river, the Ganga, the pathway to heaven,
The river, infinite in her grace, carries the soul to the Father's feet.

भागीरथी ताप कियो उपारा ।
दियो ब्रह्म तव सुरसरि धारा ॥

Bhāgīrathī tāp kiyo upārā,
Diyo Brahm tav surasari dhārā.

Bhagirathi (the Ganga) underwent great penance,
And Brahma granted her the divine flow.

जब जग जननी चल्यो हहराई ।
शम्भु जाता महं रह्यो समाई ॥

Jab jag jananī chalyō hahrāī,
Shambhū jātā mahan rahyo samaī.

When the mother of the world moved
with a loud roar,
Shambhu (Lord Shiva) left, and the great
one remained in the midst.

वर्षा पर्यंत गंगा महारानी ।
रहीं शम्भू के जाता भुलानी ॥

*Varṣā paryant Gaṅgā Mahārānī,
Rahīm̐ Shambhū ke jātā bhulānī.*

Until the rains, the Ganga, the queen, remained,
Shambhu (Lord Shiva) was there, guiding her with care.

पुनि भागीरथी शम्भुहीं ध्यायो ।
तब इक बूंद जटा से पायो ॥

Puni Bhāgīrathī Shambhūhīṁ dhyāyo,
Tab ik būnd jaṭā se pāyo.

Then Bhagirathi (the Ganga) meditated
upon Shambhu (Lord Shiva),
And from his matted hair, she received a
single drop.

ताते मातु भें त्रय धारा ।
मृत्यु लोक, नभ, अरु पातारा ॥

Tāte mātṛ bhēṁ tray dhārā,
Mṛtyu lok, nābhā, aru pāṭārā.

Then, the mother (Ganga) manifested in three streams,
Reaching the world of death, the navel, and the netherworld.

गई पाताल प्रभावती नामा ।
मन्दाकिनी गई गगन ललामा ॥

Gain pāṭāl prabhāvatī nāmā,
Mandākinī gaī gagan lalāmā.

She (Ganga) went to the netherworld, named Prabhavati,
While Mandakini (another name for the Ganga) rose to the sky, shining like a red flame.

मृत्यु लोक जाह्नवी सुहावनी ।
कलिमल हरनी अगम जग पावनि ॥

Mṛtyu lok Jāhnvī suhāvanī,
Kalimala harnī agam jag pāvanī.

The Jāhnvī (Ganga) flows through the world of death, beautiful and auspicious, She who removes the impurities of the Kali Yuga, and is the sacred purifier of the universe.

धनि मइया तब महिमा भारी ।
धर्म धुरी कलि कलुष कुठारी ॥

*Dhani Maiyā tab mahimā bhārī,
Dharmam dhurī kali kaluṣ kuṭhārī.*

Then, the glory of the blessed mother
(Ganga) was immense,
She is the destroyer of the impurities
of the Kali Yuga, the purifier of
righteousness.

मातु प्रभवति धनि मंदाकिनी ।
धनि सुर सरित सकल भयनासिनी ॥

Mātṛ prabhavati dhanī Mandākinī,
Dhani sur sarit sakal bhayanāsinī.

The mother (Ganga) arises as the blessed Mandakini,
She, the divine river, destroys all fears, revered by the gods.

पन करत निर्मल गंगा जल ।
पावत मन इच्छित अनंत फल ॥

Pan karat nirmal Gaṅgā jal,
Pāvat man icchit anant phal.

When one touches the pure waters of the Ganga,
The mind attains its desired and infinite fruits.

॥

पुरव जन्म पुण्य जब जागत ।
तबहीं ध्यान गंगा महं लागत ॥

*Purva janma puny jab jāgat,
Tabhīn dhyān Gaṅgā mahan lāgat.*

॥

When the merit of past lives awakens,
Then, the meditation on the great Ganga begins.

जई पगु सुरसरी हेतु उठावही ।
तई जगि अश्वमेघ फल पावहि ॥

Jai pag surasarī hetu uṭhāvahī,
Tae jagi aśvamegh phal pāvahi.

Those whose feet raise the divine river (Ganga),
They attain the fruit of performing the Ashwamedha sacrifice.

महा पतित जिन कहू न तारे ।
तिन तारे इक नाम तिहारे ॥

Mahā patit jin kahū na tāre,
Tin tāre ik nām tiharē.

Those who are the most sinful and cannot
be saved by anyone,
They are saved by your name alone.

शत योजन हूं से जो ध्यावहिं ।
निशचाई विष्णु लोक पद पावहीं ॥

Śat yojan hūṁ se jo dhyāvahi,
Niśchāī Viṣhṇu lok pad pāvahi.

Those who meditate from a hundred
Yojanas away,
They surely attain the feet of Lord Vishnu
in his divine realm.

नाम भजत अगणित अघ नाशै ।
विमल ज्ञान बल बुद्धि प्रकाशे ॥

Nāma bhajat agaṇit agh nāśai,
Vimal jñāna bal buddhi prakāśe.

By chanting the divine name, countless
sins are destroyed,
And pure knowledge, strength, and
intellect are illuminated.

॥ॐ॥

जिमी धन मूल धर्म अरु दाना ।
धर्म मूल गंगाजल पाना ॥

Jimi dhan mūl dharmam aru dānā,
Dharmam mūl Gaṅgājal pānā.

॥ॐ॥

Just as wealth is rooted in its source,
charity, and virtue,
Virtue is rooted in the sacred Ganga
water.

तब गुन गुनन करत दुख भाजत ।
गृह गृह सम्पति सुमति विराजत ॥

Tab gun guṇan karat dukh bhājat,
Gṛh gṛh sampati sumati virājat.

Then, virtues are praised, and suffering is removed,
In every home, wealth and good judgment shine.

गंगहि नेम सहित नित ध्यावत ।
दुर्जनहूं सज्जन पद पावत ॥

Gaṅgahi nem sahit nit dhyāvat,
Durjanhūṁ sajjan pad pāvat.

One who constantly meditates on the
Ganga with reverence,
Even the wicked attain the path of the
virtuous.

उद्दिहिन विद्या बल पावै ।
रोगी रोग मुक्त हवे जावै ॥

Uddihīn vidyā bal pāvai,
Rogī rog mukt have jāvai.

One who seeks knowledge and strength,
Becomes free from illness and suffering.

गंगा गंगा जो नर कहीं ।
भूखा नंगा कभुहुह न रहहि ॥

Gaṅgā gaṅgā jo nar kahiṁ,
Bhūkhā naṅgā kabhuhu na rahī.

He who always chants 'Ganga, Ganga,'
Shall never be hungry or naked.

निकसत ही मुख गंगा माई ।
श्रवण दाबि यम चलहिं पराई ।।

Nikusat hī mukh Gaṅgā māī,
Śravaṇ dābī yam chalahiṁ parāī.

The moment the Ganga flows from the mouth,
The sound reaches the ears, and Yama (the god of death) turns away.

महं अघिन अधमन कहं तारे ।
भए नरका के बंद किवारें ॥

Mahā aghin adhman kahān tāre,
Bhae narakā ke band kīvāre.

How can the great sinner or the wicked be saved,
When they have become bound by the gates of hell?

जो नर जपी गंग शत नामा ।
सकल सिद्धि पूरण ह्वै कामा ॥

Jo nar japī Gaṅgā śat nāmā,
Sakal siddhi pūraṇ hwaī kāmā.

One who chants the hundred names of
the Ganga,
All their desires are fulfilled, and all
achievements are realized.

सब सुख भोग परम पद पावहीं ।
आवागमन रहित ह्वै जावहीं ॥

*Sab sukh bhog param pad pāvahiṁ,
Āvāgaman rahit hwai jāvahiṁ.*

One who experiences all pleasures and
attains the supreme state,
Is liberated from the cycle of birth and
death.

धनि मइया सुरसरि सुख दैनि ।
धनि धनि तीरथ राज त्रिवेणी ।।

Dhani Maiyā surasari sukh daini,
Dhani dhani tīrath rāj triveṇī.

Blessed is the mother (Ganga), the river of the gods, who gives happiness, Blessed, blessed is the king of all pilgrimage sites, the Triveni.

ककरा ग्राम ऋषि दुर्वासा ।
सुन्दरदास गंगा कर दासा ॥

Kakarā grām ṛṣi Durvāsā,
Sundardās Gaṅgā kar dāsā.

In the village of Kakarā, the sage Durvasa,
And Sundardas, a devoted servant of the
Ganga.

जो यह पढ़े गंगा चालीसा ।
मिली भक्ति अविरल वागीसा ।।

*Jo yah paṛhe Gaṅgā chālīsā,
Milī bhakti aviral vāgīsā.*

Whoever reads the Ganga Chalisa,
Will receive unbroken devotion and the grace of the divine.

॥ चौपाई ॥

नित नए सुख सम्पति लहैं, धरें गंगा का ध्यान ।
अंत समाई सुर पुर बसल, सदर बैठी विमान ॥

संवत भुत नभ्दिशी, राम जन्म दिन चैत्र ।
पूरण चालीसा किया, हरी भक्तन हित नेत्र ॥

Nit naē sukh sampati laihain,
dharē Gaṅgā kā dhyān.
Ant samā'ī sur pur basal,
sadar baiṭhī vimān.
Samvat bhut nabdishī,
Rām janm din chaitra.
Pūraṇ chālīsā kiyā,
Harī bhaktan hit nētra.

One who meditates on the Ganga daily,
will receive new happiness and wealth.
At the end, they will reach the heavenly
abode, seated respectfully in a divine
chariot.
On the auspicious day of Ram's birth in
the Chaitra month,
Reciting the complete Ganga Chalisa, they
will earn the blessings of Lord Hari and
his devotees.

आरती श्री गंगाजी

ॐ जय गंगे माता, मैया जय गंगे माता।
जो नर तुमको ध्याता, मनवांछित फल पाता।।
ॐ जय गंगे माता।।

चन्द्र-सी ज्योति तुम्हारी, जल निर्मल आता।
शरण पड़े जो तेरी, सो नर तर जाता।।
ॐ जय गंगे माता।।

पुत्र सगर के तारे, सब जग को ज्ञाता।
कृपा दृष्टि हो तुम्हारी, त्रिभुवन सुख दाता।।
ॐ जय गंगे माता।।

एक बार जो प्राणी, शरण तेरी आता।
यम की त्रास मिटाकर, परमगति पाता।।
ॐ जय गंगे माता।।

आरती मातु तुम्हारी, जो नर नित गाता।
सेवक वही सहज में, मुक्ति को पाता।।
ॐ जय गंगे माता।।

Aarti Shri Gangaji

Om Jai Gange Mata, Maiya Jai Gange Mata
Jo Nara Tumako Dhyata, Manavanchhita Phala Pata
Om Jai Gange Mata

Chandra Si Jyoti Tumhari, Jala Nirmala Ata
Sharana Pade Jo Teri, So Nara Tara Jata
Om Jai Gange Mata

Putra Sagara Ke Tare, Saba Jaga Ko Gyata
Kripa Drishti Ho Tumhari, Tribhuvana Sukha Data
Om Jai Gange Mata

Eka Bara Jo Prani, Sharana Teri Ata
Yama Ki Trasa Mitakara, Paramagati Pata
Om Jai Gange Mata

Aarti Matu Tumhari, Jo Nara Nita Gata
Sevaka Vahi Sahaja Mein, Mukti Ko Pata
Om Jai Gange Mata

Aarti Shri Gangaji

Om, Victory to You, O Ganga Mother, Victory to You, O Ganga Mother.
The person who meditates upon You, attains all their desires.
Om, Victory to You, O Ganga Mother.

Your light is like the moon, and the water that flows from You is pure.
The person who surrenders to You, crosses all difficulties and attains salvation.
Om, Victory to You, O Ganga Mother.

You are the savior of the children of the ocean, known throughout the world.
May Your grace bestow happiness upon the three worlds.
Om, Victory to You, O Ganga Mother.

Whoever surrenders to You even once, finds refuge in You.
You remove the fear of Yama (the god of death) and lead one to the ultimate goal of salvation.
Om, Victory to You, O Ganga Mother.

The person who sings Your Aarti daily,
Naturally attains liberation by serving You.
Om, Victory to You, O Ganga Mother.

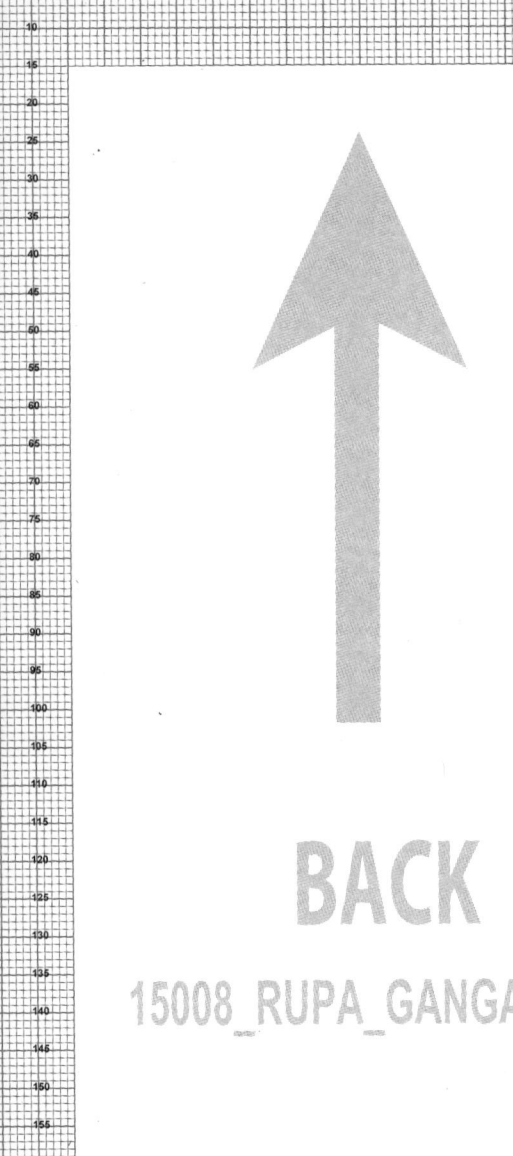